WHEN
GOD CALLS
HE
ANOINTS

CHERYL INGRAM

Edited by Anne Rose, Way with Words.
Printed in the United States of America.

When God Calls, He Anoints
ISBN: 0-9626900-0-7
Cover design and illustration by Jeff Cline.

Library of Congress Catalog Card Number: 90-83584

Unless otherwise indicated, all Scripture quotations are
taken from the *King James Version of the Bible,*
published by Thomas Nelson Inc., 1972.

Other Scripture references are taken from *The Living
Bible,* published by Tyndale House Publishers, 1962;
The Amplified Bible, published by the Zondervan
Corporation and the Lochman Foundation, 1987.

IMI Publishing Company
P.O. Box 820954
Fort Worth, Tx 76182-0954

It's the Anointing

It's the anointing
That makes the difference.
Once you've known Him
You'll never be the same.
You can't live without Him,
Once He's rested on you.
He will show you how to walk
In Jesus' name.[1]

Dedication

This book is lovingly and respectfully dedicated to my grandfather, the Rev. Ed Cox, whose anointing still inspires and challenges me, long after his promotion into heaven.

ACKNOWLEDGEMENTS

To Steve: My husband, my best friend, and the
              father of my son. Thanks for helping
              me reach beyond what I thought was
              possible.

To Billie: My mother, co-laborer, and personal
              confidant. Thanks for always insisting
              that I follow God.

To Valerie: My friend, my secretary, and a fellow
              psalmist. Thanks for your diligence
              and endurance in the midst of intense
              pressure.

TABLE OF CONTENTS

Preface

It was the spring of 1989. Our School of the Psalmist was scheduled for October, and I had about six months to prepare my teaching. Students would be attending from many countries and from all across the United States, Christians who were hungry to fulfill their callings as musicians and singers, worship leaders, recording artists, and pastors. They needed to understand their priestly role as psalmists chosen by God to lead the Body of Christ into a lifestyle of worship.

The Spirit of God spoke to my heart to teach on the subject of anointing. He said, "There will be people coming who need specific answers. They must hear from Me, or they will lose hope. The future of their ministries depends on this teaching."

As I shared this on the opening night, many began to burst into tears. One woman told me later that until that night she had wondered why she had enrolled. She had never heard of any of the teachers but felt she should attend. She and her husband were leaders in the Lutheran Church-Missouri Synod, with the responsibility of musical direction for their entire denomination. She realized that night she had to have an understanding of God's anointing to accomplish the task.

Later that evening, her roommate, whom she had just met, prayed with her to receive the baptism of the Holy Spirit. She was gloriously filled! The teaching on the anointing gave her courage to obey God.

When I first began research on the subject, I found my own understanding to be very limited. The anointing was a supernatural phenomenon I thought difficult to explain. I knew God's anointing was on my life and ministry, but how it got there, or why, was beyond me. One day, my husband handed me a small notebook saying, "Maybe something in here can help you."

The notebook was old and had the smell of vintage books. Loose papers of various sizes and colors were interspersed between neatly typed pages of notes. As I thumbed through it, I realized this had been my grandfather's sermon notebook. It was given to my husband when Papaw died in 1977. Steve had put it away for safekeeping, until the Lord prompted him to give it to me.

Each message was so full of wisdom and faith. It read like something written by E.W. Kenyon or Smith Wigglesworth. At the same time, it ministered current and relevant lessons to me.

I was shocked and amazed to find that Papaw Cox had preached sermons on subjects I have written songs about. Then the Holy Spirit began to reveal things to me about transference of anointing that have radically changed my life. Although my research has not been exhaustive, this new insight has brought a freer and more powerful flowing in the Spirit.

For weeks, I could not study my grandfather's notebook without weeping. It was the point of contact for God to reveal to me what the anointing is, how He functions in the Body of Christ, what His purpose is, and how the anointing can be increased. **I know now that this revelation is not only for psalmists, but for the whole Church Body — laymen and ministers alike.** In order for the great revival and harvest of souls to come, we must have an increase of God's anointing! As you read the next several pages, I pray—

> **...that you can know and understand the hope to which He has called you...and what is the immeasurable and unlimited and surpassing greatness of His power in and for us who believe...**
>
> **Ephesians 1:18, 19**
> **The Amplified Bible**

What Is the Anointing?

Many times we speak of a person or a service as being "so anointed." We know there is a difference by the **results** of the ministry and not by appearance, personality, or style. The anointing goes beyond superficial trappings. It allows the presence of God to move unhindered.

Perhaps you've been in a service where everyone present sensed this intangible electricity. The music was especially exciting. Even the musicians and singers felt they could play and sing no wrong notes. It seemed easy to flow in praise and worship. The hearts of the people, as well as the minister, were stirred so that salvation, healing, and deliverance began to manifest freely.

What made this service so unique? Was it the person or persons leading the service? Did some unexplainable, supernatural experience take place, or was there a set of circumstances that led to this wonderful occurrence?

The answer to these questions, of course, is the subject of this book. The anointing certainly isn't to be taken lightly, but it isn't as mystical as we have made it out to be. We can know what the anointing is. We must learn how to operate in the anointing as individuals, as ministers of the Gospel, and corporately as the Body of Christ.

It is the anointing that makes the difference. The anointing breaks the yoke of bondage. The anointing will set the captive free. The anointing brings great deliverance. A familiar passage of scripture says—

> **And it shall come to pass in that day, that his burden shall be taken away from off thy shoulder, and his yoke from off thy neck, and the yoke shall be destroyed because of the anointing.**
> **Isaiah 10:27**

Isaiah was prophesying about a time when a remnant of Israel would be set free from bondage to their enemy. He said, "the yoke shall be destroyed because of **the anointing**." Many Bible scholars believe this phrase refers to the coming of Jesus. The Hebrew word **mashah**, meaning "Messiah," and the Greek word **Chrein**, meaning "Christ," also mean "the anointed one."[2] The yoke is destroyed because of the anointed one. Acts 10:37, 38 says—

> **...that word, I say, ye know,... How God anointed Jesus of Nazareth with the Holy Ghost and with power: who went about doing good, and healing all that were oppressed of the devil; for God was with him.**

Jesus Christ—the Messiah, the Anointed One, our Redeemer—came to set men free. Everything necessary to complete God's plan of redemption and salvation for man was accomplished once and for all by Jesus. He doesn't need to die again. No more blood needs to be shed. But His ministry of deliverance still operates today through the person of the Holy Spirit. The **Anointed One** still sets the captive free by the power of the Holy Spirit operating **through** believers.

How we relate to the third person of the Trinity directly influences the anointing on our lives and ministry. Rather than depending on our own talents and/or charisma, we need to allow the Holy Spirit to work through us. The anointing can take your life, your ministry, or any service out of the natural and into the supernatural realm.

A good illustration of supernatural is that God's **super** abilities merge with our **natural** abilities to cause the miraculous! As Jim Earl Swilley wrote, "You can't live without Him, once He's rested on you. He will show you how to walk in Jesus' name."[3]

Definition of Anoint

To understand how to function in the anointing, we must first define what anointing is. Webster's Dictionary says that to anoint is—

> **to rub over with oil or an oily substance;**
> **to apply oil to as a sacred rite especially**
> **for consecration; to designate as if**
> **through the rite of anointment.**[4]

Zondervan's Bible Dictionary tells us that anointing a person or thing with oil was a common practice in the East.[5] There were, actually, three kinds of anointing commonly administered: ordinary, medical, and sacred.

Ordinary Anointing

Out of respect for a guest, people in the Middle East would wash his feet and apply cleansing perfumes and oils to his body. It was especially refreshing after long travel across the desert terrain. It was a form of hospitality.

To anoint the body with oils and perfumes was also a common part of grooming oneself. We've continued the practice today. Billions of dollars are spent each year on lotions and cosmetics.

Like the Egyptians, the Israelites used oil in burial, although less extensively. A corpse would be anointed with oil and perfumes, then wrapped in cloth. Jesus' body was wrapped in a long linen shroud. The women from Galilee watched as He was laid in the tomb. They then went home to prepare spices and ointments to embalm him—or anoint him (Luke 23:53-56, The Living Bible).

Medical Anointing

The act of anointing the sick and wounded with oil prevailed from the Old Testament priests to the New Testament believers. Other medications were often used, as well as oil.

Through the years, doctors have been the "ministers" of healing. Although medical science is continually advancing the healing process, Jesus is the ultimate healer! By His stripes we **were** healed (1 Peter 2:24)!

Just as the practice of administering salves and ointments has continued in modern medicine, so the act of anointing the sick with oil continues in the Church today.

> **Is any sick among you? Let him call for the elders of the Church; and let them pray over him, anointing him with oil in the name of the Lord: And the prayer of faith shall save the sick, and the Lord shall raise him up....**
>
> **James 5: 14, 15**

Sacred Anointing

Obviously, the sacred anointing is the focus of our study. Oil was used in Old Testament times to dedicate things or persons to God. Zondervan's Bible Dictionary says, "...they were thus set apart and empowered for a particular work in the service of God." [6]

After receiving the Lord's detailed instructions on how to build the tabernacle and how to fashion the priests' apparel, Moses was told to anoint Aaron with oil. This was a definite act of consecration, of setting apart as holy. It indicated that Aaron was to be honored and revered from that time forward. God also commanded Moses to anoint the entire tribe of Levites, all of Aaron's sons.

> **And thou shalt anoint them, as thou didst anoint their father, that they may minister unto me in the priest's office: for their anointing shall surely be an everlasting priesthood throughout their generations.**
> **Exodus 40:15**

The Lord further prescribed the dedication of the tabernacle and the instruments of worship.

> **And thou shalt take the anointing oil, and anoint the tabernacle, and all that is therein, and shalt hallow it, and all the vessels thereof: and it shall be holy.**
> **Exodus 40:9**

> **And Moses took the anointing oil, and anointed the tabernacle and all that was therein, and sanctified them.**
> **Leviticus 8:10**

Throughout Israel's history, not only were priests consecrated by anointing, but kings and prophets as well. Samuel anointed Saul—and later David—with oil as God's choice to lead Israel. Although the scriptures don't specify that oil was used on Elisha, tradition and God's commandment would indicate it. (We'll study the anointing of Elijah and Elisha in a later chapter.)

God is serious about the act of anointing with oil. **It is a holy, sacred rite of consecration. It establishes a person or thing in the service of the Lord.** Even though a person may depart from his or her calling and anointing, what has happened in the Spirit realm remains.

For instance, Saul was called to be the king, but his effectiveness deteriorated as he walked in disobedience. In jealous rages he persistently attacked David, the one chosen to replace him. Yet, David pitied Saul and would not take his life, although it seemed the most expedient action. In fact, David openly rebuked the young man who claimed he had slain Saul:

> **Why were you not afraid to stretch forth**
> **your hand to destroy the Lord's anointed?**
> **2 Samuel 1:14**
> **The Amplified Bible**

David ordered the death of the young man for taking Saul's life.

Because God is serious about setting people apart for His service, we must take the act of anointing seriously. It is not our place to judge, but to honor. God is the judge of men, and He will render to all men their just rewards of service.

Let's look again at the definition of sacred anointing. **It is an act of anointing with oil a person or thing in the service of God. They are set apart and empowered for a particular work.** To understand the anointing more completely, we need to examine two key words in this definition: "oil" and "empowered."

The Anointing Oil

In the Old Testament, **the oil was used as spiritual purification.** God directed that the priests,

11

the Tabernacle, and the vessels should be anointed with oil, or purified, so that His presence could operate freely. **The anointing oil in the Old Testament represents the Holy Spirit in the New Testament**. Before Jesus ascended to the Father, He told the disciples to wait for the promised Holy Spirit. These were born-again believers who needed the experience of baptism, not just in water, but in the Holy Ghost.

Jesus was preparing His followers for purification by the Holy Spirit, so that His presence in them could operate freely. They were instructed to wait in the upper room for the promise of the Holy Spirit. For 40 days they were in prayer, earnestly anticipating God's gift. They had separated themselves for the service of the Lord, and they were **all** gloriously filled with the Holy Spirit to **overflowing!** They were **anointed** and **purified**.

I suggest, then, that any vessel, any individual, who wants to be used by God should be baptized, **purified**, in the Holy Spirit so that they can—

> **...be a vessel set apart and useful for**
> **honorable and noble purposes,**
> **consecrated and profitable to the Master,**
> **fit and ready for any good work.**
>   **2 Timothy 2:21**
>   **The Amplified Bible**

Is this to say that not all Believers have experienced a form of **purification** unless they have been baptized in the Holy Ghost? Not at all. The experience of being born again cleanses us from all unrighteousness, and we then have a measure of the Holy Spirit **with** us. John 14:17 says that the Holy Spirit "...is **with** you, but shall be **in** you."

However, in the baptism the disciples received, which is still available for believers today, the Holy Spirit, the oil of anointing, comes on the inside of a person's spirit and fills to **overflowing**. The overflow spills out to touch other people's lives. The Holy Spirit Himself enters, purifying the spirit-man and giving **power** to be a witness of Jesus Christ.

The Anointing Means Power

Once again, the definition of sacred anointing is—

> **to dedicate things or persons to God by anointing with oil. They were thus set apart and empowered for a particular work in the service of God.** 7

We've already established that the oil represents the Holy Spirit. Jesus said to the disciples—

> **But you shall receive power (ability, efficiency, and might) when the Holy Spirit has come upon you;...**
>
> **Acts 1:8**
> **The Amplified Bible**

The word **power** used here is the Greek word **dunamis** which means "miraculous power, ability, abundance, might, strength, the working of miracles and wonderful works."8 Jesus was telling His followers that He was giving them the same abilities that He had received from the Father. The same anointing that was on Jesus would be available to **all** who would receive the **dunamis** power of the Holy Spirit.

That meant that all the great miracles and wonderful works that Jesus demonstrated could now be performed by **anyone** who would receive the baptism of His power. In fact, Jesus said—

> ...He that believeth on me, the works that
> I do shall he do also; and greater works
> than these shall he do; because I go unto
> my Father.
>
> **John 14:12**

Can you imagine that? Jesus said that we would do even **greater works** than He had done. The **Anointed One** can come inside us and fill us to overflowing with His power, so that we can lay hands on the sick and they'll recover. The blind can receive their sight. Like Jesus, we can direct the hearts of humanity to our Father, who longs to welcome them with open arms.

Those gathered in the upper room knew they had received **power**, because they spoke with tongues as the Spirit gave the utterance (Acts 2:4). Their verbal communication with the Father in an unknown language was the outward manifestation of the Spirit of God residing **inside** them. They had been anointed, **empowered**, set apart, consecrated for the work to which God had called them. The result of this anointing was that 3,000 believers were added to the Church that day! The Anointed One—through the person of the Holy Spirit—was now **inside** them, working to set the captive free!

The disciples continued to do the works of Jesus, **empowered** by the Holy Spirit. They healed the sick, raised the dead, and delivered people from bondage to the devil. You and I have the same opportunity to continue the works of Jesus. We can be baptized in the Holy Spirit. We can be **empowered**. We can be anointed to break the yoke of bondage!

The Holy Spirit, in a baptized person, purifies the spirit-man, giving power to be a witness and a representative of Jesus in the earth. A person anointed by the Holy Spirit is an ideal vessel for God's use in His good works, because God delights in one who desires to operate in the anointing. When the Spirit of God is pleased, His **power** is released.

The definition of anointing, then, can probably be summed up in one word...**power!**

Part One

Types of Anointing

Types of Anointing

Why is it that we seem to complicate the basic principles of the Christian life? We perceive the Gospel as being some great mystery, impossible to understand, when in fact God's truth is so simple. Take salvation, for instance.

Jesus, the sacrificial Lamb of God, gave His life at Calvary so that we can have complete remission (removal) of sin in our lives. Sin separates us from our Father God. We come to the Father through Jesus, by accepting Him as the Savior and Lord of our lives. It is an act of **faith**: "...by grace are ye saved through faith..." (Eph. 2:8). It is **belief** that God will do what He's promised in His Word.

Little children have no problem accepting Jesus into their hearts. They hear the Word. They believe the Word. They **act** on the Word. However, many adults try to reason it out. They think, "I can never be saved. I'm too great a sinner. I could never be forgiven." Or, "I'm not really that bad a person. I don't need to be saved." The truth is that separation from God means **separation**. Whether you are a vile sinner or a wonderful human being, you must "be born again" (John 3:3) to come to the Father.

Faith—belief in God's Word—is the foundation of every Biblical principle. If you believe God's Word and act on His Word, then the Word will work for you! Romans 10:13 says, "...**whosoever** shall call upon the name of the Lord shall be saved." That means the evil person, the good person, **whosoever!** But it takes using **faith**, acting on God's Word, to be saved.

Understanding the anointing is no different. It is a very simple truth. **It is an act of faith.** To be anointed means to be purified, set apart, and empowered for service unto God. In the next several chapters, we'll see what the Word of God says about different types of anointings. If you receive the Word about operating in the anointing, your life and ministry will be forever changed. Don't only be challenged by the Word. Be changed by the Word!

Remember, just as receiving salvation is an act of faith, so is receiving the anointing.

Chapter One
The Individual Anointing

Only selected people were anointed for service in the Old Testament. In the New Testament, Jesus made the Holy Spirit available to all believers, because every believer is called to a ministry. That ministry may not be a public or professional one, but it is of great value to the Kingdom of God. Let's look at Acts 1:8 in the Amplified Bible.

> **But you shall receive power (ability, efficiency, and might) when the Holy Spirit has come upon you, and you shall be My witnesses in Jerusalem and all Judea and Samaria and to the ends (the very bounds) of the earth.**

We've already learned that the anointing oil represents the Holy Spirit. To be anointed means to be endued with **power.** When you are born again, a portion of the Holy Spirit is **with** you, and when you are baptized in the Holy Spirit, He is **in** you (John 14:17). The **power** of the Holy Spirit fills you to overflowing, so that you reach out and minister to others.

In other words, in salvation the anointing is **with** you, and in the Holy Spirit baptism the anointing is **in** you. Every believer is anointed! First John 2:20 in the Amplified Bible says—

But you have been anointed by...the Holy One, and you all know the Truth.

Anointed for Service

Jesus said, "...you shall receive **power** (ability, efficiency, and might)..." by the Holy Spirit working in you and through you. You are more than able to be an efficient, **effective**, and **strong witness**. What does a witness do? **A witness is someone who testifies about the facts!**

My husband, Steve, and I have learned a lot about the American judicial system over the last two years. In obtaining permanent legal custody of my niece, Makenzie, we've discovered that a court must first decide if it has jurisdiction over a case. The question is, does the court have the authority or territorial right to hear the case? Once this is determined, the court will hear your story. However, you must do more than make allegations or accusations. You must present witnesses who testify to the facts. A ruling can be made only on the basis of the facts presented.

The good news of the Gospel is that Jesus gave the High Court of Heaven jurisdiction over our case. Through His shed blood, He made a way for our case to be heard. Jesus also has the authority as our advocate (or lawyer) to plead our story. We're well represented!

Then He turns around and says, "You go be witnesses!" **We've been given the responsibility of testifying to the facts...** that Jesus Christ died and rose again, and He lives now in our hearts. He desires to live in the heart of every person. We've already been given the **power** to be witnesses for Jesus Christ.

Our individual anointing is to fulfill the great commission: to go...and tell. Are you a believer? You have that anointing **with** you. Are you Spirit-filled? You have the anointing **in** you.

Fresh Oil

I believe it is imperative for every born-again believer to be baptized in the Holy Spirit. The **purification** and **anointing** that occur set us apart for service to God. Once we've been **filled** with the anointing, there are times when we'll need fresh oil. Our spiritual condition will require a fresh infilling of the Holy Spirit. We should examine our lives, daily. We should pray in the Holy Spirit, daily. But occasionally a fresh **empowering** is the essential charge we need to carry on.

Prayer To Receive the Holy Spirit

**...Repent (change your views, and purpose
to accept the will of God in your inner
selves instead of rejecting it) and be
baptized every one of you...; and you shall
receive the gift of the Holy Spirit. For the
promise [of the Holy Spirit] is to and for
you and your children, and to and for all
that are far away, [even] to as many as the
Lord our God invites and bids to come to
Himself.**

**Acts 2:38, 39
The Amplified Bible**

As with all principles of the Christian life,
receiving the baptism of the Holy Spirit is so **simple**.
Just as it is with salvation, it is an act of **faith**. It is a
free gift. Ask the Lord now to fill you with the Holy
Spirit, and the outward manifestation of this infilling
will take place. You'll begin to speak in another
language (tongue) as the Spirit gives the utterance.
On the day of Pentecost—

**...everyone present was filled with the
Holy Spirit and began speaking in
languages they didn't know, for the Holy
Spirit gave them this ability.**

**Acts 2:4
The Living Bible**

This tongue is your special prayer language or
communication with the Father God. It is a sign to
you that His **power** resides inside your spirit-man.[9]

Let's pray now.

Father God,

As your born-again child I thank you for the gift of the Holy Spirit. In Jesus' name, I ask you to fill me now. Baptize me in the Holy Ghost. I believe I receive, according to your Word, the **power** to be your witness in this earth. Thank you, Lord. I believe I receive **now**!

Now, lift your hands and begin to praise God. Speak words of love and thanksgiving to Him, and your prayer language will take over. Hallelujah!

Chapter Two
Anointing for Ministry Gifts

The anointing, or power, of God is available to every believer. All can have the ability to be strong, effective witnesses for Jesus Christ by being filled to overflowing with the Holy Spirit. Every Christian has the responsibility to testify that Jesus Christ is Lord to the glory of God the Father. That is the ministry of every believer. However, in addition to this individual anointing, God has ordained another anointing.

Although God does not have favorites, for He is no respecter of persons, He does call certain individuals for a specific function in the work of ministering. That call is always followed by a special anointing, or power, to accomplish it. When God asks you to do a service for Him, He will provide you with everything you need to get the job done. In fact, He's all that you need. He's your source and supply. First Thessalonians 5:24 says, "Faithful is He that calleth you, who also will do it."

The Fivefold Gifts

The callings of God for the work of ministering are outlined in Ephesians 4:11 and First Corinthians 12:28. They are often referred to as the fivefold ministry gifts or "offices." The Amplified Bible says that God has appointed or given men to the Church for His own use. That purpose is to equip the saints, to build up the Body of Christ, to do the work of ministering until we all come into a unity, or oneness, in the faith. We've got a way to go to achieve that.

Until we realize that unity, God will continue to call people to an area of particular service. The five different gifts are outlined as follows.

1. **Apostles** - "sent ones," special messengers used in building missions and churches.

2. **Prophets** - inspired preachers who bring forth revelation through preaching of the Word and in prophetic utterance.

3. **Evangelists** - preachers of the Gospel, traveling missionaries who have a special ability to lead others in salvation.

4. **Pastors** - leaders who care for God's people as a shepherd would his flock (also known as bishops, overseers, or elders).

5. **Teachers** - leaders who explain and instruct in the Word of God.

All of these offices incorporate the teaching and preaching of the Word of God. Besides these, five other ministries may accompany the gifts of the fivefold ministries or may operate independently.

They may be called the supportive gifts.

Supportive Gifts

1. **The Working of Miracles** - invocation of acts that could come only by the hand of God; the impossible becoming possible.

2. **The Gift of Healing** - ability to minister health to the sick through laying on of hands and/or a word of knowledge (i.e., known by the the Spirit and not by the natural man).

3. **The Ministry of Helps** - special gift for assisting day-to-day, natural functions of the ministry (for example, ushers, altar workers, or staff).

4. **The Gift of Administration** - skill in business affairs and in getting others to work together.

5. **Speaking in Different Tongues** - conveying a message in tongues by the inspiration of the Holy Spirit, in a public meeting. One who has this gift should also be able to interpret the tongue or word of the Lord.

Whether you've been called as an apostle, a prophet, an evangelist, a pastor, or a teacher, or you minister through miracles, healing, helps, administration, or speaking in tongues, it is the Holy Spirit who **empowers** you. He equips you with a special anointing to accomplish your part. Operating in your gift requires an act of faith. God always honors faith because He has—

> **...not given us the spirit of fear; but of power, and of love, and of a sound mind.**
> **2 Timothy 1:7**

Faith in God produces **power**! Faith in the **gift** God has given you produces **power** (miraculous power, ability, abundance, might, strength, the working of miracles and wonderful works) to operate in the **gift**. Don't ever doubt that.

Stir Up the Gift

Timothy must have doubted that he was anointed to function as an evangelist. That's why Paul wrote to remind him to... "stir up the gift of God" (2 Tim. 1:6). Paul told him to keep alive the inner fire that drives one to serve God. In other words, it was Timothy's own responsibility to stir up the gift in his life.

Stirring up the gift brings the anointing. How do we stir it up? By praying in the Holy Ghost, by operating in our individual anointing (witnessing), and by doing the works of the ministry. Get about your Father's business: "...Do the work...make full proof of thy ministry" (2 Tim. 4:5). We cannot allow the gift to lie dormant, or the anointing will be suppressed. So don't back away from your anointing; stir it up!

Chapter Three
The Psalmist Anointing

When God first called me to be a psalmist, I had no idea what a psalmist was. I knew that David was a psalmist and that a book in the Bible was called the Psalms. It recorded 150 psalms, or songs, by different authors, including David. I had always thought of them as poetry.

My husband and I had been professional musicians for several years, working out of a recording studio in Central Florida. We also organized and traveled with Alpenglow, a contemporary Christian music group. We recorded on the House Top label, sponsored by the Christian Broadcasting Network, and we were regulars on "The 700 Club" and other CBN programs.

Our ministry has always been in and around music. We understood the special way music was used to promote the Gospel, and we saw many thousands of young people come to Jesus through our music. But the psalmist ministry was still a great mystery.

Just like me, there are many musicians and singers today who don't know what a psalmist is. Many have outstanding ministries. Some are true worshipers who operate in a strong anointing to lead others into God's presence. But they don't understand their calling. God doesn't want us to be ignorant. He's ready and willing to show us the truth. John 16:13 says the Holy Ghost is the Teacher of the Church and will show us **all** things.

That being so, I decided to separate myself unto God and allow Him to teach me what a psalmist is. At the time, my husband was the director of the Kenneth Copeland Band and I was a backup vocalist. Steve was arranging many of Brother Copeland's albums, and we were growing in our faith.

I didn't know anyone else who knew about the subject, so I relied, totally, on the Holy Spirit. For almost a year, when I wasn't traveling with the Copelands I went to school with the Holy Ghost in my living room. I would study the Word and listen to tapes. But most of the time I simply worshiped the Lord. Through the worship, God began to teach me basic principles that radically changed my music ministry.

One of those principles is that **music is a spiritual force before it is an audible force.** The Creator, Himself, lives inside creative people. His creativeness resides inside a born-again musician or singer. There are notes that have still never been sung or played, because we haven't realized that the Creator wants to transmit them through us.

Great power, great anointing exists in music as a spiritual force. On the wings of music, healing and deliverance take place. The devil and his demons tremble at the sound of those notes, and strongholds in people's lives begin to fall!

I discovered that the Greater One lived inside me. At the sound of my voice, rivers of living water could flow through me to set the captives free! **I was called to be used to usher in the presence of God!**

What Is a Psalmist?

This was all very exciting, to say the least, but I still didn't know what a psalmist is. When I asked the Holy Spirit to show me, He surprised me by sending me to the dictionary. I didn't think that was very spiritual, but I obeyed. Webster's Dictionary defines—

> **psalmist**—a writer or composer of sacred songs.
>
> **psalmody** - the act, practice, or art of singing psalms in worship.[10]

I laughed when I read these definitions. I thought, "That's it? That's all a psalmist is? One who writes or sings sacred songs." Why do we complicate the Gospel? Why do we think that God's ways are so mysterious when His truth is very simple?

According to the definition, I certainly qualified as a psalmist. Then the Lord showed me that to Him a psalmist is one who writes and sings the "song of the Lord," that is, the new song that He's placed inside him or her (2 Chron. 29:27). I had to learn to release those sounds from inside my spirit-man. I discovered that the anointing, the power given me by the Holy Spirit, would help me to sing brand new songs I had never rehearsed, which came fresh from my spirit-man.

God showed me the great importance of the psalmist ministry. The song He has given me is to be used in His worship—to glorify and exalt Him, to lead others into His presence, and to minister to them. I discovered that psalmists are positioned on the front lines of the Army of God, because praise and worship are weapons of warfare. Just as Elisha called for the minstrel (2 Kings 3:15), I too could stir the heart of the prophet to speak forth the word of God. This gift not only ministers to others, but also it brings delight and good pleasure to my Father.

Is It a Ministry Gift?

With this fresh revelation about the psalmist ministry, the scriptures in Ephesians 4 and First Corinthians 12 outlining the fivefold ministry gifts became increasingly troublesome to me. I asked the Lord, "If the psalmist anointing is as important as you've shown me, then why isn't it listed with the ministry gifts? Why aren't they called the sixfold ministry gifts?"

In my search for the answer, I read articles by some who placed the singer and musician in the area of helps. It certainly is that. But the psalmist ministry does more than prepare the people's hearts to receive the Word. **It is the Word through music!**

During the time of preparation for my own psalmist calling, I attended a conference on the various functions of ministries. After one session, I went to the speaker and introduced myself. I told him the Lord had called me to the work of a psalmist, and I needed to know why it wasn't listed with the fivefold gifts. "That's a good question," he said. "I've never been asked that before. Let's just pray together, right now, and ask God to show us."

For what seemed an eternity we stood there. Then suddenly he said, "I know! It's because **the psalmist is all five!**"

That went off in my spirit like a stick of dynamite. However, I had to make sure it lined up with the Word. As I prayed and studied about it, I became convinced. The psalmist ministry is actually the **spirit** of all five gifts. First Corinthians 12:28-30 specifically says that no one functions in **all** five simultaneously, so the psalmist doesn't literally **operate** in all five ministry gifts. But a person called to the office of a psalmist can and should function in at least one of the fivefold ministries. A psalmist will be stronger in one gift and will probably be called to that office where he excels.

The Office of the Psalmist

The "office" of a psalmist denotes authority, leadership, and reponsibility. Webster's Dictionary, in one of its definitions, says that an office is..."a prescribed form or **service of worship.**"[11] That beautifully describes the vocation of a psalmist: **one who is called to the service of worship**. It requires more than an interest. It demands a permanent servitude.

A psalmist may be called as an **apostle**, whose role is to be sent as a special messenger. Psalmists can, in fact, go where other ministers cannot. Music will be received when the strict preaching or teaching of the Word will not be. Many psalmists have been used around the world on the missionary field to build churches.

The psalmist is anointed in the **prophetic**. In the Old Testament the same word meaning "seer" was used for both the prophet and the singer. Most of the prophetic books were originally sung, not just spoken. A prophecy on the wings of music has a great anointing. It cuts through into the spirit world, because it has spiritual power, even **before** it is audible. The song of the Lord comes fresh, under the leading and anointing of the Holy Spirit. It can be a song of praise and worship, or it can be prophetic.

The ministry of musical **evangelism**, of course, has been in practice for a long time. Typically, we put a music team together to draw a crowd and prepare the people to receive the "preaching" of the Word. However, a psalmist has the ability to preach the Word through music, and by the anointing, the presence of God is manifest. When God's presence is there, salvation is the result. Therefore, the psalmist serves as an evangelist, one who has the special ability to lead others to Christ.

Many psalmists function as **pastors**. They may be senior pastors or music directors or praise and worship leaders. Their objective as psalmists is to lead others into worship, but they also shepherd people. A true pastor has a tremendous ability to care for people. During worship he or she is especially inclined to sense needs and minister to them.

Finally, the gift of the **teacher** can operate either through a psalmist's songs or through traditional instruction. When I write songs, they are based on an inspired idea that I study out of the Word. My songs could read like sermons, but of course I attempt to make them poetic. Steve and I also teach through public speaking in churches and in the School of the Psalmist.

Since I've been teaching that the psalmist ministry is the **spirit** of the fivefold, many ministers have shared with me how they could never justify that they were called to the service of worship and the office of a teacher or a pastor at the same time. They now say this new understanding has set them free.

The Psalmist/Supportive Gifts

Along with the five ministry gifts, the other five supportive gifts also operate through a psalmist. There can be a manifestation of **healing and miracles**. Chapters 10 and 11 of Nehemiah outline the responsibilities of the singers and musicians, who were of the priestly tribe of Levites. A psalmist ministers in the area of **helps**, for a music program involves much work, whether in a church setting or otherwise. Most of it is not very glamorous. The singers were also in charge of the business affairs of the tabernacle, so a psalmist can be gifted in **administration**. And, finally, a psalmist can sing forth a **word in tongues** and interpret that message.

Are All Psalmists Called to the Fivefold?

I do believe that a person called to the office of the psalmist is called within the fivefold ministry and this is recognized by leadership. A singer or musician who does not have this calling is probably used instead in the area of psalmody.

Let me explain. **Just as a person can have the gift of prophecy without being called to the office of a prophet, a person can operate in psalmody (the act, practice, or art of singing psalms in worship) without being called to the office of a psalmist.** Such a person could be anyone from a member of the congregation singing in corporate worship, to a choir member, to any other member of the worship team. These people will not be called to leadership positions but may operate more strongly in the supportive gifts, such as helps or administration. They may even have an occasional song in tongues and interpretation. These supportive gifts should not be misinterpreted as a calling into the "office" of a psalmist.

Personal Note

By no means do I intend to elevate the calling of the psalmist above any other ministry gift. In essence, a calling into the fivefold ministry complements the psalmist anointing and vice versa. They are not in conflict; neither is one greater than the other. Over the years, we have religiously come to view the music ministry as subordinate to the other gifts, when in actuality there is a marriage of callings and anointings.

Much strife has been generated in churches where a minister of music feels his gift is treated with less importance than that of a pastor, or teacher, or other leader. Conversely, the pastor or some other leader suspects the music minister of seeking to elevate his gift above the rest. Both positions are in error.

As we'll learn in the next chapter, we must learn to respect one another's callings and anointings. When we flow in unity, Jesus Christ is lifted up and people's needs are met. Thank God for **all** the ministry gifts, and thank God for anointed psalmists who lead us into God's presence. In His presence is fullness of joy!

Chapter Four
The Corporate Anointing

My husband Steve and I greatly respect the anointed ministry of Kenneth Copeland, as a prophet and a teacher and a psalmist. His impartation to us has been priceless. It was Brother Copeland who prophesied several years ago that Steve would begin to teach new musical laws that the music world had never known. Since then, we've learned many things from the Spirit of God that we now teach to other singers and musicians in our School of the Psalmist.

The six years we spent working full time at Kenneth Copeland Ministries were like Bible school for us. We were learning the Word before thousands of people, and when we made a mistake, it was obvious. I learned much about operating in the anointing. Many times, during the music, the anointing would be so strong that I would know what song Brother Copeland would sing next. Even if the song wasn't on our list, I would sense in my spirit what the Holy Spirit was telling him. When he would operate in the word of knowledge and healings would manifest, I knew in my spirit, **before** he spoke, what he would say. Of course, I either prayed or sang in the Spirit, supporting what he was doing, all the while anticipating his next move.

One day I asked Brother Copeland how I knew what he was going to do and say next. He answered me this way: "Cheryl, that is the corporate anointing. That anointing is available to every person on our stage. Obviously, not everyone takes advantage of it. But you have. If everyone would flow in the corporate anointing, the Holy Spirit could do whatever he wants."

Body Power

The word corporate comes from the Latin word **corporatus**, which means "to make into a body." Webster's Dictionary defines **corporate** as—

> **formed into an association and endowed by law with the rights and liabilities of an individual; of or relating to a whole composed of individuals.**[12]

Doesn't that sound like the Body of Christ? We are a group of individuals, coming together to form one whole. Romans 12:4-6 in the Living Bible says—

> **Just as there are many parts to our bodies, so it is with Christ's body. We are all parts of it, and it takes every one of us to make it complete, for we each have different work to do. So we belong to each other, and each needs all the others. God has given each of us the ability to do certain things well.**

And Ephesians 4:16 (The Living Bible) says—

> **...Christ who is the Head of his body, the church. Under his direction the whole**

**body is fitted together perfectly, and each
part in its own special way helps the other
parts, so that the whole body is healthy
and growing and full of love.**

That is a glorious picture of the Church. If
corporate means **body** and **anointing** means
power, then the Church of Jesus Christ should be
operating in **body power**. In the corporate anointing
the Spirit of God is unleashed to do the miraculous.
The same power that Jesus possessed is now
distributed to the whole Body, each of us doing his or
her part. Every time the "parts" come together, that
power should be exhibited.

Unity

Why do we seldom see the anointing operate
corporately? Because of strife and jealousy and ego
and pride. We get our feelings hurt when our
ministry or our gift is not recognized. We get
opinionated, thinking that one ministry is more
important than another. And, the spirit of
intimidation is rampant in the Church — in the local
church and in many ministries. People are so easily
overawed by the anointing in others, or they instead
try to intimidate others because of their position or
calling.

It's wrong. God isn't pleased, and He'll never
work to maximum capacity as long as these "evil
works" operate in the Body of Christ. We're
supposed to prefer one another in love, esteeming

the other better than ourselves, being a support and encouragement to one another.

> **For wherever there is jealousy (envy) and contention (rivalry and selfish ambition), there will also be confusion (unrest, disharmony, rebellion) and all sorts of evil and vile practices.**
>
> **James 3:16**
> **The Amplified Bible**

The anointing cannot and will not ever operate under these conditions. **The dunamis power of God will not be released in the Church, until God's people repent of sin and walk together in unity.** Thank God, we can be forgiven. Even Paul said, "...the Lord shall deliver me from every evil work..." (2 Tim. 4:18) Too much is at stake for the Church of God to allow disunity. There is a world going to hell. There are needs to be met. Jesus prayed in chapter 17 of John that we would be one even as He and the Father are **one.**

When we flow together in love, our individual anointings merge with our callings in the ministry gifts to form a perfect union in the Spirit. No one ministry is exalted above the other. There are no superstars, except Jesus. God uses men who will humble themselves and submit themselves to His purpose, which is that **He** must be glorified. There is a **reward** for unity.

Look at Psalm 133.

> **Behold, how good and pleasant it is for**

brethren to dwell together in unity! It is like the precious ointment upon the head, that ran down upon the beard, even Aaron's beard: that went down to the skirts of his garments; As the dew of Hermon, and as the dew that descended upon the mountains of Zion: for there the Lord commanded the blessing, even life for evermore.

When the Body of Christ is walking in harmony, the **ointment** (the anointing oil; the Holy Spirit, the anointing) comes from the **head** (who is Jesus, the head of the Church) and flows down over the rest of the Body. The anointing flows from Jesus to **all** the parts of the Body. No one is left out. As surely as you can count on the dew falling to the ground, you can count on the anointing falling on the Church (Zion), when the brethren dwell in unity. The result is that **God commands the blessing on Zion (the Church)!**

God's Blessing! God's Anointing! God's Presence!

No lack can stand when God's blessing is present. No sickness or disease can remain when God's anointing is present. No problem is so great that God's presence cannot solve it. That's the reward of the dunamis power of God.

The corporate anointing is an anointing on individuals who come together at one time, as the Body, fitly joined together, for the purpose of glorifying and worshiping God. When God's presence is manifest, salvation, healing, deliverance, and miracles occur. This can happen through the music. It can happen through the preaching. It can happen through any ministry.

When God's Body simply worships Him, without strife, respecting one another's functions and callings, the anointing of God flows and the supernatural takes over. God's **super** abilities merge with our **natural** abilities to cause the miraculous.

Chapter Five
Measures of Anointing

Whenever I've heard someone talk about different "levels" of anointing, I've wondered what they meant. The Bible, actually, discloses "measures," meaning degrees or amounts of anointing. The Greek word **metron** used in the New Testament means "of length or capacity."[13]

John described Jesus as the perfect man, the Son of God and the Word made flesh.

> **...God's Spirit is upon him without measure or limit.**
>
> **John 3:34**
> **The Living Bible**

If Jesus, being perfect, had the Holy Spirit (or the power of God or the anointing) without measure, then I must presume that, because I am imperfect, **I have the anointing with measure.** There were no limits on Jesus' anointing, but there are limits on my anointing.

> **But unto everyone of us is given grace according to the measure of the gift of Christ.**
>
> **Ephesians 4:7**

Having a **measure** of anointing that is different in

amount or level from others might appear, at first, to be unfair. But God knows the thoughts and intents of every person. Hebrews 2:4 tells us that He gives "gifts" or "distributions" of the Holy Ghost **according to His own will.** There are many reasons why one person's life and ministry are more anointed than another, but the basic reason is because **it's as the Spirit wills.**

It is not up to us to question God's ways but to do what He says and to receive. When we obey His Word, we'll walk through various levels of anointing.

The First Level: The Individual Anointing

Thank God! **Every believer has a measure of the anointing.** We have the Holy Spirit **with** us when we're born again (John 14:17). Then when we receive the Baptism of the Holy Spirit, we receive that "dunamis" explosive power **in** us to be witnesses for Jesus Christ. This measure or level or degree or amount of anointing is available on an **individual** basis and **is the foundational level for all other anointings.**

The Second Level: Anointing for Ministry Gifts

The individual level of anointing is followed by the callings and gifts of ministry within the Body of Christ. God is sovereign, and He calls and anoints people, just because He's God.

When He calls us, He gives us **a measure of anointing** for the call, and our responsibility is to be diligent in the "...effectual working in the measure..." (Eph. 4:16). **The "effectual working" simply means to work our measure of anointing effectively.** We must be productive in every area of ministry that the Word instructs for our calling. When we've done everything God has outlined in the Word concerning our area of ministry, then our ministry gift will be fully developed. Therefore, our measure of anointing is fully developed. That's the "...effectual working in the measure..."[14]

In Second Corinthians 10, Paul talks about operating in the measure that God has given. He stresses the importance of staying within the confines of your measure and ministering with excellence there, until God enlarges your area of responsibility (2 Cor. 10:12-16). **With an increase of responsibility comes an increase or greater measure of anointing.**

The Third Level: The Corporate Anointing

> **...the head, even Christ: from whom the whole body fitly joined together and compacted by that which every joint supplieth, according to the effectual working in the measure of every part, maketh increase of the body unto the edifying of itself in love.**
>
> **Ephesians 4:15,16**

When we have reached our fullest potential as individual believers and ministers of the Gospel, the whole Body of Christ is increased. That connotes measurement. If something can increase, it can also decrease. Our objective, of course, is not to go backward, but forward, toward the prize or reward of our high calling. Our goal is described in Ephesians 4:13.

> **Till we all come in the unity of the faith, and of the knowledge of the Son of God, unto a perfect man, unto the measure of the stature of the fullness of Christ:...**

Jesus had **all the gifts and all the ministries** operating through Him. He was the **perfect man**. Now, the Word says, He's the head of the Church, the Body of Christ. He's given these gifts, or distributed measures of anointings, throughout the Body, so that **we** can do the works. Our objective is to strive for that perfection, as a **Body**. No, we're not perfect as individuals. But as a Body, fitly joined together and flowing in unity, we can achieve **the measure** of Christ's anointing.

What is that measure? One with no limitation. Jesus Christ had the anointing without measure. That's why, I believe, **the corporate anointing is the highest level that can be achieved.** The signs and wonders following Jesus' ministry (such as healing, deliverance, and miracles) will follow believers who are joined together in harmony, in faith, and in the knowledge of who they are in Christ. When the Body of Christ achieves this, we become the **perfect man** that Jesus was, and we flow in His anointing. There is nothing impossible with Jesus' anointing.

You might be asking, "Can the Church really achieve this perfection?" Certainly we have a long way to go. We've seen the measure of Christ's anointing operating in very limited fashion, so far. Rather than being discouraged by our own ineptness, we need to be encouraged by our achievements. Walls are coming down in the natural and in the spiritual. Walls of religious thinking are coming down, and people around the world are more open today than ever before to the truth of God's Word. People are being born again and filled with the Holy Spirit in enormous numbers. Healings and miracles are occurring everywhere, in all denominations, through ministers and ordinary laymen. God is moving by His Spirit all over the earth!

The anointing on the Church is now stronger than at any other time in our history. As the spirit of darkness increases and this age draws to a close, God's anointing continues to increase. The Church of God must, daily, draw on that anointing. How do we draw on the anointing? By flowing in our individual anointings, by obeying our callings and "effectually working in the measure," and by joining our gifts together as one **perfect man** operating without limitation.

When we do what the Word says, the anointing will increase. More and more of God's power will be poured out over all the earth. More signs and wonders will follow us, and God will be glorified until, finally, Jesus returns for a fully mature Church, ready to rule and reign with Him. Hallelujah!

How the Anointing Is Increased

The corporate anointing is increased when the whole Body of Christ is unified, flowing in their individual gifts, striving to be the **perfect man** Ephesians 4:13 describes. The question remains, how do we cause the anointing to increase at the individual and ministerial levels? There are several actions that work in conjunction with one another.

Association with others who operate in a strong anointing is the first action. Every Christian needs to be planted in a local church, with an anointed pastor who allows the Spirit of God to move freely. A pastor will teach you and guide you in the ways of the Lord. He will protect you from error and correct you when you make a mistake. **Your pastor's anointing is a covering of protection over your life.** Make sure you are submitted to an anointed man of God!

We are products of our environment. We will reap the seeds sown into our lives. Therefore, we should associate with ministries of like calling who are known for their integrity and excellence. **Giving of yourself to serve another person's ministry allows his or her anointing to come on you.** You've heard the term "guilty by association." The concept is true of the anointing. Your anointing will increase when you associate with others who operate in a stronger anointing.

The second action that causes the anointing to increase is **prayer and fasting.** Remember that to be anointed means to be endued with **power** (dunamis power, miraculous workings of the Holy Spirit). Prayer brings the anointing.

> ...The earnest (heartfelt, continued) prayer of a righteous man makes tremendous power available [dynamic in its working].
>
> **James 5:16**
> **The Amplified Bible**

Paul admonished us to pray "in the Spirit" or to "pray in tongues."

> I thank God that I "speak in tongues" privately more than any of the rest of you... [but] I will do both, I will pray in unknown tongues and also in ordinary language that everyone understands.
> **I Cor. 14:18 & 14:15**
> **The Living Bible**

Praying in tongues is a direct communication by the Holy Spirit to the Father. It bypasses the devil, our minds, our physical sensation, and our emotions. It is the fastest way to focus on the presence of God, who resides inside your spirit-man.

Fasting should always be accompanied by prayer; otherwise you're just going without food for a season. The purpose of denying your body of food is to allow your spirit to become more sensitive to the presence of God. You starve your flesh to feed your spirit. Of course, your flesh benefits from fasting. If you fast correctly, your body can be cleansed from impurities. Fasting requires wisdom and great discipline, but it brings a powerful anointing. Some scripture references are Matthew 4:2, Matthew 6:18, Acts 13:3, Acts 14:23.

Meditation in the Word will also increase the anointing. To **meditate** means, "to reflect or muse on something; to ponder it; to contemplate (to view or consider with continued attention)."[15] Read the Word and reflect on the Truth. Ponder the scriptures in your heart. Give the Word of God your continued attention and the Word will saturate your spirit. There is an anointing on the Word.

Another way to increase the anointing is through a **lifestyle of praise and worship.** We enter into worship through praise. Praise requires physical action. The Hebrews have seven words for praise, all of which demonstrate action of the flesh.

> **Barak**—to kneel before the Lord in reverence and honor.
>
> **Yodah** and **Towdah**—to extend the hands in praise.
>
> **Zamar**—to play instuments and sing.
>
> **Shabach**—to shout unto God with the voice of triumph while clapping.
>
> **Halal**—to rave; to boast about the Lord;

to be wild until clamorously foolish
(dancing is included here).

Tehillah - to praise until God's
presence is manifested; the highest form
of praise. [16]

Placing demands on our flesh to praise God
(kneeling, lifting our hands, singing, shouting,
clapping, dancing, rejoicing) causes God to **delight** in
our praise so much that **He "inhabits" our praises.**
He dwells in the midst of them (Psalms 22:3). God
says, "They look like they are enjoying themselves so
much. I like the party they're throwing. I think I'll
join them." God is a Jew, you know. He likes a good
party! That's when the highest form of praise,
tehillah, occurs. God's manifested presence brings the
anointing.

When God's presence comes, your spirit takes
control of your flesh and begins to worship Him.
**You see, you don't worship God with your flesh.
You worship Him with your spirit.** John 4:24
says—

> **God is a Spirit: and they that worship him
> must worship him in spirit and in truth.**

But often your flesh has to get involved before
your spirit can. Didn't Jesus say to His disciples,
"...the spirit indeed is willing, but the flesh is weak "
(Matt. 26:41)? Don't be afraid of "getting in the
flesh" when you praise. Your flesh is required to
praise God. Praise causes the anointing. Purpose in

your heart to make praise and worship a lifestyle and not merely an event you participate in.

Finally, the last action that will increase the anointing is **long periods of silence**. Ecclesiastes 3:7 points out—

> **A time to rend, and a time to sew; a time to keep silence, and a time to speak;...**

There are times when we need to be quiet and listen to the voice of God for instruction and exhortation. **Putting faith and action behind God's direction increases the anointing**. In Section II of this book, we'll learn how to hear the voice of the Lord.

If a person will follow these actions—association, prayer and fasting, meditation in the Word, a lifestyle of praise and worship, and long periods of silence— the anointing is bound to increase.

So far, we've discussed measures of anointing on an individual, on the ministry gifts, and on the Church. We've seen that the anointing can be increased and decreased. In this area of measures of anointing, we still need to define several terminologies.

Drawing on the Anointing

The first is an area already mentioned—drawing on the anointing. The woman with the issue of blood pressed through the crowd to touch Jesus. Although many people were touching Him, the woman used her faith to draw from Jesus. He said He felt virtue, or **power**, leave Him. The anointing for healing manifested and made her whole, because she did three things: **she believed** that Jesus was anointed, **she put a demand** of faith on the anointing, and **she was committed** to the ministry she saw in Jesus. These are three steps to drawing on the anointing.

First of all, she believed that Jesus was anointed. Whether we're in a large meeting or we're involved in one-on-one ministry, we must accept, believe in, and receive the anointing from the one who is ministering. If we don't believe that person is anointed, then we cannot expect the Holy Spirit to operate through him or her on our behalf. Nothing will happen. The Holy Spirit is restricted from manifesting until we exercise our faith that He is present **in** other people.

Second, we have to put a demand of faith on the anointing. Faith is believing that something is, before you see it. Faith is a knowing in your spirit that it's already done. A demand of faith means to insist, to require, to persist without relenting, because your faith says you already have what you need. **But people can only demand to the point the ministry is developed**.

Third, we must commit ourselves to that person's ministry. Apart from a sovereign move of God, if you don't trust that person's ministry, you cannot receive from him or her. We need to have faith that God has called and anointed this person for this service. **The**

degree to which we commit is the degree to which we will receive. Commitment is not always financial, although it plays a significant part. One must be convinced of the calling and anointing on the minister. So, drawing on the anointing is directly related to the faith level of the person being ministered to.

To conclude, we draw on the anointing (1) by believing that the minister is anointed, (2) by putting a demand of faith on his or her anointing, and (3) by making a commitment to his or her ministry. When we draw on the anointing, just like the woman with the issue of blood, we'll receive what we need.

The Pouring-Out of Anointing

Acts 2 reveals the classic story of Pentecost. Everyone in the upper room was filled with the Holy Ghost and spoke in new languages given them by the Spirit. Peter, addressing the crowd who witnessed the event, quoted the prophet Joel.

> **And it shall come to pass in the last days, saith God, I will pour out of my spirit upon all flesh: and your sons and your daughters shall prophesy, and your young men shall see visions, and your old men shall dream dreams: And on my servants and on my handmaidens I will pour out in those days of my Spirit;...**
>
> **Acts 2:17, 18**

Just as the anointing oil was poured out over the head of Aaron, God said He would **pour out** His

Holy Spirit on all flesh. Acts 10:45 says that "...on the Gentiles also was **poured out** the gift of the Holy Ghost."

I envision God holding a huge pitcher and **pouring out** spiritual oil. This **outpouring** is the best way to describe what happens in the Spirit. You become completely drenched in the Holy Ghost. The anointing is so strong that you're more aware of spiritual things than natural things.

Why doesn't it happen all the time? Remember, it's as the **Spirit wills** (Heb. 2:4). God has His own reasons for moving at particular times. Also, I believe our faith level, or expectancy, can make the atmosphere conducive for the Holy Spirit to be **poured out.**

The Falling of the Anointing

Growing up in a pentecostal church, I was taught that the Holy Ghost never entered a room—He "**fell**"! And when He would fall, wild and crazy things would happen. People would shout and scream and dance. Every service, the same little old lady would get up and dance and shake all the hairpins out of the glory curls piled on top of her head. When I married a good ol' Southern Baptist boy, he taught me that the Holy Spirit can fall in different ways. The Spirit is a perfect gentleman, and He will never impose Himself on someone uninvited.

The Word of God very definitely speaks of the Holy Spirit "falling." In Luke 3:22, heaven was opened and the Holy Spirit **descended** like a dove on Jesus. Immediately after, He was tempted by the devil, and then He began His public ministry. Not only was this anointing an acknowledgement that Jesus was the Son of God, but also He received **empowerment** for the work before Him. Acts 2:3 says a sound from heaven as a rushing mighty wind **sat on** (or settled on) each of them. In Acts 10, the Holy Ghost **fell** on everyone, including the Gentiles. And Peter explained that the Holy Ghost was **sent down** from heaven (I Peter 1:12). So the anointing can and does "fall" on individuals and on whole congregations.

The Lifting of the Anointing

The Holy Spirit means **power**—dunamis power, like a stick of dynamite exploding. Because we're made up of spirit, soul (mind, will, and emotion), and body, we can sense this **power** in all three areas.

Our spirit man receives the anointing—spirit to Spirit. With enough experience in spiritual things, you can feel the anointing in your spirit. **Our soul has difficulty receiving the anointing**. It takes an act of our will to receive, but our mind tells us lies. The mind is foreign to spiritual things. That's why we have to learn how to shut our minds down at times.

When we do receive an empowering, our emotions may react. We might cry, we might laugh, we might dance. Sometimes we can feel the power in our flesh. I've heard ministers say they felt heat or a tingling sensation in their hands as they prayed for people. No matter if we feel the Holy Spirit or not; He still has to be received by faith.

In any event, **our bodies can handle just so much of this power.** Our spirits can receive unlimited anointing, but our spirits live in our bodies. It's wonderful to know that one day we'll discard these earth suits, and then our spirits will operate in the supernatural, totally unrestricted. Until that happens, God knows when we've had enough and the Spirit will "**lift.**"

There are times and seasons for a pouring out and falling of the anointing. As the Spirit wills, He moves on people. Only He knows the hearts and minds and needs of everyone, so He alone can anoint for specific occasions. When He's finished with the ministry of the moment, He will "**lift**" the anointing.

Another way the Holy Spirit will lift is when He is grieved. He is the third person of the Trinity and must be treated with respect. When we do not honor Him, when we get out of the Spirit, or when we're in strife, the Holy Spirit is grieved and He will leave. Any anointing that has been present will "**lift.**"

Flowing with the Anointing

A good friend of mine, Dennis Burke, was explaining how the anointing flows. He gave this example. Rivers flow. If you want to ride a river, you get into a canoe or boat and go with the current. The

flow of the river will take you where you need to go.

It is not wise to paddle upstream, against the current. You are very likely to encounter great turbulence that causes you to capsize. So it is with the Holy Spirit. **Get in the flow of where He wants to go.** Stay sensitive to the moving of the anointing.

Summary

A measure of anointing has been given to every Christian at the born-again experience and at Holy Spirit baptism. Distributions of anointing are also given to the ministry gifts. These anointings can increase by association, prayer, meditation in the Word, a lifestyle of praise and worship, and long periods of silence. The corporate anointing is increased when the whole Body of Christ joins together in their individual and ministerial anointings to flow in the measure of Jesus' anointing, which is the highest level that can be achieved. Finally, we've defined several terminologies associated with measures of anointing: drawing on the anointing; the pouring out, falling, and lifting of the anointing; and flowing with the anointing.

Part Two

How To Know Your Calling

How To Know Your Calling

My mother says that she knew I was called to the ministry when I was still in her womb. By the time I was 13, I was born again and filled with the Spirit, and at the age of 14 I had an encounter with God that has proven to be life-changing. Kneeling by my bed praying, I heard a voice say to me, "Through thee, my child, I shall work wonders!" I looked behind me to see who said it. There was no one there.

I believe I heard an audible voice. No one else was in the room with me to verify it, but it was so real that I expected to see Jesus standing there.

Then the Spirit of God began to speak to me in my spirit (a different sound than I had heard before) about the call of God on my life. His instructions were so clear and specific that when I shared them with my mother she immediately took me to our pastor. They both realized I had a supernatural experience. Word of it spread through the church. My Sunday school teacher cried with thanksgiving, and everyone was blessed that God had spoken to "their" little girl.

In the years that followed, I ran from the call, selfishly pursuing my own interests. Even though I was living a carnal and sinful life, I couldn't deny that I had been given a "higher" calling. At 19, I came to the point of total surrender. I asked Jesus to forgive me of my sins, I was filled afresh and anew with His Spirit, and I set out to obey the call.

The Calling

My personal experience is typical and not so typical in several ways. It's typical in that the call on my life was with me from conception. Everything else about us is formed at conception: our appearance, our personality (to a great extent), even how long we'll live our lives are decided before we're born. **I believe that God chooses people from the beginning to "...summon them to a particular activity, employment or office."** [17] The Apostle Paul obviously believed this.

> **... it pleased God, who separated me from my mother's womb, and called me by his grace, To reveal his Son in me, that I might preach him among the heathen;...**
> **Galatians 1:15, 16**

The Amplified Bible says he "...had chosen and set me apart even before I was born and had called me..."

The Knowing

Though the calling is with us when we're born, it may take us years to become aware of it. My realization came in my youth, which is typical of many people's experiences. Some, however, do not know of the call till much later in life. Whether earlier or later, the Father chooses an appointed time to disclose the direction of your calling.

The Surrender

What we do with God's direction totally depends on our own will. We make the decision to obey the call or to reject it. Failing to act on the call is also to reject it. Many people have good intentions, but they get preoccupied or they wait for the right circumstances, and they never totally surrender. Others like me from selfishness or fear never act on the call. I thank God, He brought me to a place of surrender, and I responded with **"Yes!"** I was miserable outside God's will, and my years in the ministry since, though not always easy, have been irreplaceably rewarding.

How Are We Called?

Not so typical was my experience of hearing an audible voice. Moses heard the Lord speak to him. So did Samuel and Paul. An angel appeared to Zechariah and to Mary with the word of the Lord, and Joseph saw an angel in a dream. These supernatural happenings still occur today, but they are rare. Most people receive direction through the word of God, either by an inward witness, a prophetic word, and/or by transference of anointing.

Chapter Six
The Inward Witness

The Word of God is our final authority. If our beliefs, calling or direction do not line up with the Word, then we're already in error. By daily studying the Bible, meditating on the Word, listening to the Word (through preaching) and, then, acting on God's Word, we allow the Lord to speak to us. He may not speak to us in our flesh. We probably won't hear Him with our natural ears. He most likely will not speak to us in our minds, because "...the carnal [fleshly] mind is enmity against God..." (Romans 8:7). Our minds try to reason or argue things. God cannot be reasoned in the natural. John says that God is a **spirit** who must be worshiped in **spirit** and in truth.

Therefore, we have to learn to hear God speaking to us in our own spirits. We must train our spiritual "ears" to hear the voice of the Lord. That doesn't mean we become some crazy weirdo who's always hearing voices. We pray for discernment, making sure we hear God's voice and not the evil one's. We rebuke the enemy from lying to us or deceiving us from the truth. And, we base anything we hear on the Word of God. Does it line up with God's Word? God will never contradict His Word. Satan will only tell a partial truth. Does this word glorify self, God, or someone else? [18]

Where Is Our Spirit?

> ...Jesus stood and cried, saying, If any man
> thirst, let him come unto me, and drink.
> He that believeth on me, as the scriptures
> hath said, out of his belly shall flow rivers
> of living water. (But this spake he of the
> Spirit, which they that believed on him
> should receive...)
>
> John 7:37-39

The Amplified and the Living Bible both say,
"from the innermost—or inmost—being." Jesus was
saying that the Holy Spirit or the **anointing will
flow from within our inner beings**, which is the
area of the heart or stomach (the center of the
body). Our spirits, the real "us," live inside our flesh.
It is our spirits that are reborn. Our flesh and our
mind become renewed after our spirit is reborn. The
Holy Spirit also baptizes us on the **inside** of our
spirits. God comes to live within our spirits. He
abides in us! If He's in us, He can talk to us!

> Hereby know we that we dwell in him, and
> he in us, because he hath given us of his
> Spirit.
>
> 1 John 4:13

> ...And hereby we know that he abideth in
> us by the Spirit which he hath given us.
>
> 1 John 3:24

> And because ye are sons, God has sent
> forth the Spirit of his Son into your
> hearts, crying, Abba, Father.
>
> Galatians 4:6

God is our Father, who longs to fellowship with us. He wants to communicate with His sons and daughters, and He does so Spirit to spirit. His Holy Spirit speaks to us inside our spirits, where He lives. We train our spirits to hear His voice by praying (in the Spirit) and grounding ourselves in His Word. **The anointing abides in us.** He can teach us. He can give us direction. He can warn us of things to come.

> **But the anointing which ye have received of him abideth in you, and ye need not that any man teach you: but as the same anointing teacheth you of all things, and is truth, and is no lie, and even as it hath taught you, ye shall abide in him.**
>
> **1 John 2:27**

The Holy Spirit Is Our Witness

In Chapter One, we learned that we have an individual anointing to be witnesses for Jesus Christ. A witness is someone who testifies about the facts. We testify of what God has done for us, leading others into this glorious experience of salvation. In the same way, **the Holy Spirit is our witness.** Romans 8:16 says the Spirit bears **witness** with our spirit. First John 5:10 says, "He that believeth on the Son of God hath a **witness** in himself." In the New International Version it says, "...has this **testimony** in his **heart.**"

Our witness, the Holy Spirit, testifies to our own spirits and to the Father God. He reminds us, "Yes, you are born again, you are filled with My Spirit.

You are called with a holy calling." To the high court of heaven, He speaks our case. He tells the Lord, "They are born again and filled with your Spirit. You have called them with a holy calling. These are the facts, Father."

He's our witness and He lives inside us. We can be assured that our Lord is communicating with our spirits and then back to the throne on our behalf. When the enemy tries to lie and discourage us from our call, the Holy Spirit, our witness, begins to give testimony—not allegations, not hearsay, but **facts** that prove what God has done in our hearts!

We can actually **feel** His presence in our hearts. I know it isn't good to let your emotions rule your spiritual actions, but it's good to feel the Spirit of God inside your spirit. This feeling is often described as a warmth, tingling, or burning sensation. After Jesus had arisen from the dead, he appeared walking on the road with two men. They didn't recognize Him until afterward.

> **...they said one to another, Did not our heart burn within us, while he talked with us by the way, and while he opened to us the scriptures?**
>
> **Luke 24:32**

They felt something that they described as a "burning" inside their spirits. They had an inward witness that testified to their spirits about Jesus' true identity. When the Lord speaks to you concerning direction or calling, the Holy Spirit, your witness, will begin to testify inside you. You may even **feel** the anointing.

Our Intercessor and Our Partner

The Holy Spirit is our inward witness. We can hear his voice, not with our natural ears or minds, but in our spirits. We can also feel the anointing. Sometimes we feel a turmoil in our spirits. We don't know how to pray or what to ask for. That's when the Holy Spirit takes on another role as our witness. **He becomes our intercessor.** He pleads our case before the Father. He presents the facts so that we get a fair judgment. He pleads in line with God's will. When we don't know God's will, our inward witness does.

> **Likewise the Spirit also helpeth our infirmities: for we know not what we should pray for as we ought: but the Spirit itself maketh intercession for us with groanings which cannot be uttered. And he that searches the hearts knoweth what is the mind of the Spirit, because he maketh intercession for the saints according to the will of God.**
> **Romans 8:26, 27**

The inward witness will direct us on a path or through a door that is God's will for us. We never have to worry about how things will work out when we know without a doubt that we've heard from God. He will never lead us without His divine protection. I like how the Amplified says it:

> **We are assured and know that [God being a partner in their labor] all things work together and are [fitting into a plan] for good to and for those who love God and are called according to [His] design and purpose.**
>
> **Romans 8:28**

It's important not to be frustrated if you can't hear God speaking to you. He's there, whether you hear or feel Him. He's listening. He's interceding, because **He's your partner**. Your purpose is His purpose, and His purpose is yours. But He knows God's **will**. God's will involves timing. Our Father knows our maturity level and our ability to handle information. He's wise enough to withhold information from us until we're ready for it.

The Still Small Voice

Wouldn't it be wonderful if we all had an explosive supernatural manifestation of the voice of God? It would be great if we could hear an audible voice or see and hear an angel. There would be no question about our calling. The prophet Elijah went up onto the mountain because he wanted to see God. First, God came to him through the wind, then through an earthquake, and finally through the fire. But he didn't hear God in any of them. Elijah heard God in the **still small voice**.

You can have a supernatural explosion right inside your spirit. You can **know** the call of God on your life by the inward witness. In fact, **the inward**

witness is the most credible knowing of what God has called you to. It doesn't matter what other people's opinions are. You have heard from God.

When Paul knew he had been called to preach to the Gentiles, he said, "...immediately I conferred not with flesh and blood:..." (Gal. 1:16). People will often try to talk you out of your calling. Paul knew what he had to do and spent the next three years developing and preparing his gift.

I'm not telling you to ignore good counsel. Just make sure that counsel is from God. Do as Mary, the mother of Jesus, did. When she knew she was pregnant, she immediately went to someone who was more pregnant than she was—Elizabeth! When God calls you, **go to someone who is more pregnant with that call than you are.** They will encourage you and build you up. They'll give you guidance backed by their prayerful support, because they have also heard from the inward witness.

Chapter Seven
A Prophetic Word

When God calls you to a specific area of ministry, others will begin to recognize and receive it. They will bear witness in their own spirits of what God has spoken in your spirit. How do they recognize it? Because they see spiritual action or fruit or signs resulting from the call. **The Lord will confirm His word to you with signs following** (Mark 16:20). Your ministry will become fruit-bearing, and others will see the fruit. This is a confirmation that the call of God is on your life.

A "Word" of Prophecy

Another area of confirmation comes by a word of prophecy. One or more persons may single you out and speak God's word over your calling. Webster's Dictionary defines prophecy as an inspired declaration of divine will and purpose; and a declaration of something to come (prediction).[19] Zondervan's Bible Dictionary explains prophecy as the delivering of a message for God.[20] The role of the prophet is based on Deuteronomy 18:18:

> **I will raise them up a Prophet from**
> **among their brethren, like unto thee, and**
> **will put my words in his mouth; and he**
> **shall speak unto them all that I shall**
> **command him.**

God was speaking to Moses when He said He'd raise up a prophet "like unto thee." The prophet would be a friend to God, like Moses. He would speak to Him on a personal and intimate level. Every true prophet thereafter was patterned after Moses' relationship to the Father. The prophet became the voice of God speaking to the people. A true prophet was judged by the fact that his prophecy came to pass. In New Testament times, a word of prophecy (God's direction) continued through individuals who now had the benefit of the outpouring and baptism in the Holy Spirit. Paul wrote—

> **This charge I commit unto thee, son**
> **Timothy, according to the prophecies**
> **which went before on thee, that thou by**
> **them mightest war a good warfare;...**
> **1 Timothy 1:18**

> **Do not neglect the gift which is in you,**
> **[that special inward endowment] which**
> **was directly imparted to you [by the Holy**
> **Spirit] by prophetic utterance when the**
> **elders laid their hands upon you [at your**
> **ordination].**
> **1 Timothy 4:14**
> **The Amplified Bible**

A word of prophecy also came by inspiration of the Holy Spirit to Barnabas and Saul. "As they ministered to the Lord, and fasted, the **Holy Ghost said,** Separate me Barnabas and Saul **for the work whereunto I have called them**" (Acts 13:2). How

76

did the Holy Ghost say it? Through individuals, prophets, and teachers who were ministering and fasting.

Prophetic Utterance Today

The Holy Spirit still uses people to declare divine will and purpose and to give predictions and instruction. God can use anyone to speak forth His word if he or she is ministering and fasting and flowing in the Holy Spirit. But the gift of prophecy is usually given to certain individuals who are anointed in that area (I Cor. 12:10). The ministry calling of the prophet is to preach with revealed knowledge the truth of God's word. The gift of prophecy will operate in his or her ministry.

It's wonderful when God speaks by prophetic utterance. We become excited when we realize God cares about us on such a personal level that He would give someone a word for us.

I believe in personal prophecy. I operate in words of prophecy in my ministry, speaking and singing forth God's word to different people as He directs. I worked for a prophet, Kenneth Copeland, for six years. However, I want to strongly emphasize that **our intense desire to hear the voice of God can often lead to gross error.** Some churches are now allowing their entire service to be dominated by prophetic gifts. Everyone has a word for everyone, and they base their actions on these personal words. Some people have been terribly wounded and deceived because they trusted in a so-called word from God.

Steps to Receiving a Prophetic Word

There are at least five ways to assure that a word of prophecy is accurate. First, we must **have confidence in the calling and anointing of the person delivering the message.** Even if we don't know the person, we must recognize his or her gift and trust his or her reputation of ministry to be one of holiness and virtue. We can know this by the inward witness. Our spirit will bear witness with the person's spirit. Unless you trust the one giving the word, you won't receive from God.

Second, **a prophetic utterance should be spoken before other witnesses who can judge its accuracy.** If a person wants to give you a word in private, right away I'd question if he or she is sent by God. When I have a word for someone, I make sure the pastor or some other spiritual authority is present. Under these circumstances a person will more carefully guard his or her words. There is less room for error.

Third, **a true word from God will correct without condemning.** Romans 8:1 says, "There is therefore now no condemnation to them which are in Christ Jesus,..." Prophecy will exhort, edify, and encourage while it gives instruction.

Fourth, **it must always line up with the Word of God.** If it opposes God's Word, obviously it's inaccurate.

Finally, **a word of prophecy should confirm what is already in your spirit.**

God will have spoken to you, by the inward witness, about your calling and direction. The message from God validates, publicly, what you already know. If the word is a prediction of things to come in the future, pray about it. Your inward witness, the Holy Spirit, will confirm or reject the word. **Your inward witness is the most accurate judge of a true word of prophecy.**

Above all, **it's important not to base your calling or direction solely on a prophetic word.** You act when you have scriptural basis and a **knowing** in your spirit. You don't need a word of prophecy, although it's thrilling when it comes. In the last 11 years of my ministry, I've received many words. Most have been from God. A few have not. I always judge them by these five steps: (1) Do I have confidence in the person giving the word? (2) Was it given before witnesses to judge? (3) Did it exhort? (4) Did it line up with the Word? (5) Did I get an inward witness?

Right and Wrong Prophecy

The following are two examples of personal prophecy I have received. The first came after I had spent a year in preparation for the psalmist ministry in which I now operate. I had not shared with anyone, except my husband, what God had shown me. In a meeting with 10,000 believers, Kenneth Copeland called me forward and said—

> **And in the name of Jesus, according to obedience to His command, I set my hands upon you tonight, and the Lord instructed me to say this to you, "From this night forward you are set apart unto the music ministry of the psalmist that you have desired and sought for so diligently. And it will be a thing of beauty and joy and peace and life, not only to many, many thousand upon thousands of people, but to you and your family and to all of those that are close to you..."**

There was an anointing on Brother Copeland that everyone present sensed. I recognized this and received the word, because I trusted the integrity of his life in God. It was given before thousands of witnesses, it exhorted and encouraged me, it did not contradict scripture, and, above all, it confirmed what I already knew in my spirit. God was publicly declaring my ministry through a human vessel.

The second word is in stark contrast to the first. Our staff refers to it as my "scuba-diving dog" prophecy. We had been to this church several times, experiencing good crowds and excellent ministry. Unknown to us, the church had become involved in a school of prophecy that taught that all believers can and should give words to one another.

We noticed the crowd was very small and predominately female. Steve and I ministered for about two hours in music, teaching and praying for people. I was totally drained when I turned the service over to the pastor and sat on the front row.

At this point the pastor's wife felt there were several people who had a word for us, and she began calling them out. They formed a line in the front of the church. The first lady to take the microphone said something to this effect:

> Cheryl, the whole time you were
> ministering tonight I could see in the
> spirit this little bitty dog. It was a—what
> do you call that little tiny dog? (Then she
> called out to a friend in the audience.)
> (So-and-so) what is that dog that
> (So-and-so) has? That's the dog I saw.
> Anyway, this dog was under the water and
> it was just swimming all around. Then the
> dog realized that it had this thing on its
> mouth. What are those things that scuba
> divers wear to help them breathe? Well,
> whatever that is, that's what the dog had
> on its mouth, and the dog saw that it
> could breathe, so it just relaxed and
> looked at all the wonders of the deep.
> And God wants you to relax and breathe.

I thought for a minute, "This is New Year's Day. They're probably kidding." And I almost said, "This is a joke, right? You are putting me on. You're too funny!" But I realized they were very serious. One by one they gave us similar words. An hour and a half later, the last word came from the pastor's wife:

> **Cheryl, I know you have a son and you
> have your niece now, but I'm seeing in the
> spirit growth for your family. I see you
> with five children.**

I could not hold it in any longer. I blurted out, "Oh, my God," and everyone laughed. I wanted to say, "I rebuke you in the name of Jesus! I bind those words in Jesus' name!" But Steve and I politely sat through it until they dismissed. That was our mistake. We should have stopped it after the first one.

One pastor friend who heard me tell this story said, "If you're a little tiny dog, then you aren't going to have five children. You are going to have a litter!" We make jokes, but it's a sad state of affairs when people become so deceived.

With this word, there was no anointing present. I thought they were joking. I did not know anything about the people's walk with God, nor did I bear witness in my spirit they were speaking from God. The word was given before other witnesses, but it did not exhort and encourage. I was insulted to be compared to a dog.

The word had no scriptural basis, and certainly did not confirm what God had spoken to me. That woman may have seen me as a little tiny dog, but I see myself as a giant in God's Kingdom. And Steve and I have had much conversation about our family size. Five children are not what we see!

Thank God, there are people who do hear from God and speak forth a word accurately. Thank God, a word is confirmed by the inward witness. Thank God, He chooses to publicly declare what He's shown us. **But we should never seek words from God. The written Word of God is always our final authority.** We should base our life and calling on scripture first, then the inward witness. Finally, if a prophetic word does come, we're blessed. If it doesn't come, we're still blessed. With or without a prophetic word, we **know** what God has spoken.

Chapter Eight
Transference of Anointing

My maternal grandfather, the Rev. Ed Cox, began his public ministry in 1935. He already had a growing family when he and my grandmother were born again and filled with the Holy Spirit. Their life together took a dramatic change. Soon afterward, he accepted God's call to preach the Gospel. That decision set in motion a spiritual anointing that has and will affect our family forever.

Papaw Cox was called to the office of a prophet and a pastor. He was blessed with a special artistic ability, which he used to paint a large chart. The chart looked like a banner, stretching 20 feet across to make a graphically historical picture of the Bible. It would take him several weeks to teach from Genesis to Revelation, and people were intrigued by his revelation knowledge of the scriptures. Through his teaching, he prophesied that Israel would become a nation, many years before this actually occurred in 1948.

Ed and Delia Cox pastored many churches in Kentucky, Louisiana, Tennessee, West Virginia, and Michigan, but the one I remember most was in Detroit, where I grew up. It was an inner-city church, with the parsonage right next door. An empty church building holds an incredible fascination for children.

The grandchildren used to play church. One would sing, one would preach, one would take the offering, and one would get saved.

The real thing, of course, was even better. Our church had lively, exciting, hand-clapping, foot-stomping music. I recall with fond memories my grandfather, who was an anointed psalmist, leading the congregation as he sang in his deep, rich voice. We children used to love watching all the grownups have such a good time in the Lord.

My Papaw and Granny lived a long, full, productive life in the ministry. When it was time for them to go on to be with Jesus, Papaw went first. They told my grandmother he was gone, and she took it very calmly. She lay down on my mother's bed to rest, went into a coma, and died a few hours later. We buried them together. What a fitting end to a marriage partnership dedicated to the high calling of ministry.

It wasn't until many years after their deaths that my grandfather's personal preaching notebook came into my hands. As I read through his sermon notes, I was awed by his depth of wisdom and spiritual insight and amazed at a peculiar familiarity about them. Papaw had preached sermons on subjects I have written songs about. Two of them are the title songs of my recent recordings, "Follow The Light" and "Stir It Up." This notebook was about 40 years old, yet it seemed I had interjected these subjects myself. They looked like **my** notes! Turning each page, tears rolled down my cheeks. I wept, partly because of missing my grandfather so much, but mostly because of the impact of what had been transferred to me.

The Lord took me back, in the Spirit, to a time when I was 20 years old. My grandfather transferred his anointing to me. It was a short time before Papaw and Granny passed away. I spent a week asking him questions and going over different points in the Word. I was so hungry for the things of God, so desirous to fulfill the call on my life. My grandfather was the type that, when you asked him a question, two hours later he would still be answering it. He loved an audience, and I was a captive one. We literally spent hours sharing together.

At the end of this week my grandfather told me that he recognized the call on my life, and it was time for him to pass his mantle. He said he had hoped it would go to one of his sons, but that didn't look probable, and, even though I was a girl and unmarried, I was God's choice. He had learned not to question God.

He prayed a simple prayer asking God to give me a godly husband who would serve with me in the ministry. He prayed for his anointing to operate through me. No firecrackers went off. No one shouted. The three of us, my grandparents and I, just sat there quietly realizing something supernatural had occurred in the spirit.

Transference

The full meaning of that transference did not dawn on me until many years later, when I read my grandfather's sermon notes for the first time. In fact, I hadn't thought about it in years. I somehow sensed my Papaw's "presence" with me, but I could never explain it. So, I purposed to find out what all of this meant.

I knew there was quite a bit of teaching on "curses" being passed down through generations. Of course, Jesus bore the curse so that we wouldn't have to, and through His blood any curse is broken. What about anointings being passed from one generation to another? What does the Word of God have to say about that?

I discovered that **transference is both a confirmation of your calling and a spiritual impartation.** To transfer means to "cause to pass from one to another" and—

> **impart** - to give or grant from one's store of abundance: transmit.
>
> **transmit** - to send or **transfer** from one person or place to another; to cause or allow to spread. [21]

There are basically three different methods of impartation: (1) laying on hands, (2) transference by association, and (3) passing a mantle.

The Laying On of Hands

> As they ministered to the Lord, and
> fasted, the Holy Ghost said, Separate me
> Barnabas and Saul for the work whereunto
> I have called them. And when they had
> fasted and prayed, and laid their hands on
> them, they sent them away. So they, being
> sent forth by the Holy Ghost, departed...
> **Acts 13:2-4**

> Neglect not the gift that is in thee, which
> was given thee by prophecy, with the
> laying on of the hands of the presbytery.
> **1 Tim. 4:14**

In Acts, the prophets and teachers had gathered, fasting and praying, for the purpose of publicly **acknowledging** the call on Barnabas and Saul. A word of prophecy came forth, and they laid hands on them, signifying authority being given by the Holy Ghost. Paul wrote to Timothy that he should "stir up" the gift of the evangelist that was **confirmed to him by prophecy with the laying on of hands by the elders.** Why do you suppose laying on of hands was significant?

Historically in the Old Testament, the act of laying on of hands symbolized the parental bestowal of inheritance rights. An example is in Genesis 48, where Jacob was on his death bed. His son Joseph had married an Egyptian, and Jacob wanted to make sure Joseph's two sons received his covenant blessing. He placed his hands on their heads to confer on them their portions of the inheritance.

Laying on of hands was also used in dedicating an animal for sacrifice. The ceremony transferred the sin and guilt from the person to the animal. God received the animal with the sin, thereby freeing the person.

The act of laying hands on a person's head represented as well the transference of the gifts and rights of an office. The Levites in the tabernacle transferred service to other Levites.

In the New Testament, laying on hands symbolized the bestowal of blessings and benediction, the restoration of health, the reception of the Holy Spirit in baptism, and the transference of the gifts and rights of an office. [22]

Thus, the laying on of hands is an outward indication of a spiritual impartation. **In the area of gifts and callings, what is passed on is power (anointing), authority, knowledge, and insight.** Besides a confirmation, then, laying on hands also signifies the transference of one person's gifts and anointing to another. This happens "in the Spirit." A spiritual **empowering** is imparted.

To have hands laid on you means that you are already called by God, and your qualifications and anointing have been recognized by others in the Church. It is a sending forth. Your ministry is publicly sanctioned by the Church, and **you become accountable, not only to God but also to the Church for your calling.** Your **responsibility** to fulfill your calling is not only to God but to the Church, as well. That's why Paul told Timothy not to neglect the gift he received "with the laying on of the hands of the Presbytery."

Who Should Lay Hands?

The **presbytery** means the elders of the Church. These are **seasoned men and women with proven ministries themselves.** Their own experience qualifies them to transfer a spiritual impartation. Adam Clarke in his commentary warns elders against flippantly using the act of laying on of hands:

> **But, O ye rulers of the Church! be**
> **careful, as ye shall answer it to God,**
> **never lay hands on the head of a man**
> **whom ye have not just reason to believe**
> **God has called to the work; and whose**
> **eye is single, and whose heart is pure. Let**
> **none be sent to teach Christianity, who**
> **have not experienced it to be the power of**
> **God to the salvation of their own souls. If**
> **ye do, though they have your authority**
> **they never can have the blessing nor the**
> **approbation of God.** [23]

Conversely, we should be cautious of whom we allow to lay hands on us. Do they have proven, reliable ministries of integrity? Remember, it is an act of sanctioning and transferring of gifts. If possible, an elder whose calling is like yours should lay hands on you. The same type of anointing will be transferred to help you fulfill your calling.

Often in charismatic and Full Gospel circles laying on hands is used so commonly that its significance is underplayed. However, it is a serious and important indication of your calling. Therefore, give it serious prayer. The Holy Spirit will guide you to the persons who should lay hands on you. Their spirits will bear witness of what God has shown you in your spirit. They will want to give a public recognition of your calling. Don't try to force someone to lay hands on your head. Let it be a mutual knowing from the Holy Ghost that He has called you and now is sending you forth to do the work of the ministry.

Transference by Association

In Chapter Five we learned that one way the anointing can be increased is by association. **To identify with and submit yourself to another person's ministry places you under his or her anointing.** Much can be learned through someone else's expertise and experience, but in the Spirit, the same anointing in which that person flows becomes available to you. His or her anointing may even follow you, long after you have left that church or ministry, which is why it is vitally important to pray about where you are submitted.

You may have noticed that often, when someone serves another minister, he or she imitates characteristics, mannerisms, and even personality. Though not always consciously, the one serving will walk like, talk like, dress like, and even look like the minister. Sometimes it's difficult to tell their voices apart on a tape. The reason is identification and association. The minister's anointing is transmitted (allowed to spread) to the other temporarily. Eventually, the one serving will develop his or her own characteristics and personality—and his or her own anointing.

Transference by association can work in conjunction with the laying on of hands and anointing with oil. Two primary examples of this are Moses to Joshua and Elijah to Elisha. Joshua was Moses' faithful assistant. He walked in Moses' shadow until the time for his elder to be with God. Then Joshua moved out in his own power and authority. Deuteronomy 34:9 in the Amplified Bible says—

> **And Joshua son of Nun was full of the spirit of wisdom, for Moses had laid hands upon him: so the Israelites listened to him and did as the Lord commanded Moses.**

Likewise, Elisha left everything he had to follow Elijah. God instructed Elijah to anoint Elisha as prophet in his place.

> **...anoint Hazael to be king over Syria. And anoint Jehu son of Nimshi to be king over Israel, and anoint Elisha son of Shaphat of Abel-meholah to be prophet in your place.**
>
> **1 Kings 19:15, 16**
> **The Amplified Bible**

Although the Word doesn't specifically say that Elijah used oil to anoint Elisha, we assume so because of tradition and previous commandments to use anointing oil. Also, we find later that anointing oil was used on the two kings who were mentioned in this passage.

Whether by laying on of hands or anointing with oil, both Joshua and Elisha still received anointing through identification and association. Each was in a period of training under an elder, walking with the man of God until he was ready for his own authority. Joshua and Elisha became powerful leaders in their own right, but not until each had submitted to God's recognized and anointed vessel.

A point from Chapter Six, the Inward Witness, bears repeating here. When you become pregnant with a calling or a vision, get around someone who is more pregnant with it than you are. Mary went to be with her aunt, Elizabeth, who was pregnant with John the Baptist. Elizabeth didn't question Mary's mission and anointing. She confirmed it! **Submitting yourself to a "like" ministry of high integrity will increase your anointing and will cause an anointing to be transferred to you.**

Passing the Mantle

> As they were walking along, talking,
> suddenly a chariot of fire, drawn by horses
> of fire, appeared and drove between them,
> separating them, and Elijah was carried
> away by a whirl-wind into heaven. Elisha
> saw it and cried out, "My father! My
> father! The Chariot of Israel and the

charioteers!" As they disappeared from
sight he tore his robe. Then he picked up
Elijah's cloak [mantle in KJV] and
returned to the bank of the Jordan River,
and struck the water with it. "Where is
the Lord God of Elijah?" he cried out.
And the water parted and Elijah went
across! When the young prophets of
Jericho saw what had happened, they
exclaimed, "The spirit of Elijah rests upon
Elisha!" And they went to meet him and
greeted him respectfully.

2 Kings 2:11-15
The Living Bible

The preceding is the classic story of Elijah passing
his mantle to Elisha. How did the prophets of Jericho
recognize Elisha's new anointing? They saw him
carrying Elijah's mantle. With the mantle, Elisha
parted the water, just as Elijah had done a short time
before. The same power that Elijah had now
operated through Elisha.

Elijah's mantle represented his anointing. To
be anointed means to be empowered by the Holy
Spirit, to be set apart and consecrated for service
unto God. The Lord had told Elijah to anoint Elisha
(2 Kings 19:16) to replace him as prophet. In other
words, God wanted his empowering to be transferred
to Elisha. The Word says Elijah—

...departed thence, and found Elisha ...and
Elijah passed by him, and cast his mantle
upon him.

1 Kings 19:19

This gesture symbolized that the anointing was transferred. How do we know? In most instances in the Bible, the word **mantle** simply means "a loose sleeveless garment worn over clothes; a cloak; something that covers, enfolds or envelops." [24] In all the verses dealing with Elijah's mantle, the Hebrew word includes **glory** in its description.[25] (See 1 Kings 19:19, 2 Kings 2:8,13,14.) The word **glory** means—

> **praise, honor, or distinction;** renown,[26] and
> the manifestation of man's commendable
> qualities, such as wisdom, righteousness,
> self-control, or **ability.** [27]

Elijah did more than throw his coat over Elisha. He gave Elisha his own glory! He honored Elisha with his abilities as a prophet of God. Elisha understood the importance of the mantle. Second Kings 2:13 says, **"He took up also the mantle** of Elijah..." Elisha was prepared, through his association with the prophet, to take up his anointing. **The anointing can be passed, but it must also be taken up.** In most cases passing a mantle has to do with one minister's death and another's carrying on or taking up the mantle.

Who Receives a Mantle?

Jesus gave his glory to His disciples and, through them, to all who would believe on Him.

> **And the glory which thou gavest me I**
> **have given them; that they may be one,**
> **even as we are one:...**
>
> **John 17:22**

Jesus' anointing is distributed throughout the Body of Christ. We receive a measure of His anointing when we take up His mantle at new birth. The passing of the mantle also occurs through association with a ministry and through family members. **God sovereignly chooses people to take up a ministry mantle, but the desire of the heart** is also essential. If you are unwilling to carry the anointing, or if you are apathetic to the blessing, the anointing will pass you by and go to another person.

For instance, by tradition Esau as the oldest son should have received his father's blessing. However, he sold his birthright to his younger brother, Jacob, "...and went on about his business, indifferent to the loss of the rights he had thrown away" (Genesis 25:34, The Living Bible).

The same happens in families today. I believe it is God's will to continue ministry anointings from one generation to another. What stops that continuance is a lack of desire to take up the mantle. Some might argue that perhaps the call of God is not on members of succeeding generations, and that point is well taken. Nonetheless, the anointing can skip one or more generations. It can also be transmitted (caused to spread) to more than one member in a generation.

Double Portion

It is possible for the anointing to increase as the mantle is passed. Elisha was bold enough to ask,

"...I pray thee, let **a double portion of thy spirit** be upon me" (2 Kings 2:9). Elisha desired twice as much prophetic power. The double portion he referred to was the same blessing given to a first-born son. In Jewish families all the sons received a blessing, but the oldest received his portion plus a share of all the combined portions of the other sons. Elisha was like a son to Elijah. He asked for not only what was due him but also the double portion.

Elijah replied that the request could be granted only if Elisha could see into the Spirit as Elijah was taken up in the whirlwind. This indicates that the things of the Spirit must be perceived through spiritual eyes. Elisha did see it and cried, "My father! My father!" (2 Kings 2:12), as he realized his desire had been granted.

If we have a desire to move and operate in the power of the Holy Ghost, God will increase the portion of anointing that we have received.

My grandfather, Ed Cox, had a strong anointing when he passed the mantle to me. The offices of the prophet and psalmist in which he flowed set many people free. I took up the mantle, and now, through my prophetic psalmist ministry, I have already ministered to millions more people than my Papaw did in his whole lifetime. Our music and teaching tapes are all over the world. My husband and I have ministered in many foreign countries, and through the medium of television, we've been able to reach the multitudes. Just as Elisha did twice as many miracles as Elijah, we can believe God for a double portion of anointing!

Chapter Nine
When God Calls, He Anoints

The oil of anointing of the Holy Spirit represents **power** to accomplish what God has called us to. All believers have been given a measure of anointing, at the individual level, to be witnesses for Jesus Christ. Beyond this, God calls people to various ministry gifts that help build up and edify the Church.

All of these gifts, working corporately as one Body united in faith and purpose, equal the measure of anointing that was on Jesus. There were no limits on Jesus' anointing. That's why the corporate anointing is the strongest power in the earth today. When the Church of Jesus Christ realizes the miraculous dunamis power that is **now** available to be demonstrated, no evil can stand in our way. No sickness or disease will function in our members. We'll be doing the works of Jesus and even greater works. The anointing will break the yoke of bondage. The anointing will set the captive free!

Obey the Call

It is a holy calling to be God's representative in the earth. There is no higher calling. God equips you with everything you need to accomplish the call, but **until you take a step of faith to obey and walk in the call, God's anointing cannot operate.**

Whether you feel qualified or not has little to do with it. God isn't necessarily calling talented or qualified people. At the time He calls you, your talents and abilities may be lacking. You may **feel** incapable of handling the call. But, if you'll be faithful, God's anointing—His **power**—will increase your natural abilities. Remember, God's **super** abilities merge with our **natural** abilities to cause the **supernatural**.

God calls faithful people. Being faithful means doing the best you can with your natural abilities. We need to know our calling, study the Word of God, perfect our craft, and work at our skill. The anointing will then take over to help us be "reliable and faithful men who will be competent and qualified..." (2 Tim. 2:2, The Amplified Bible).

Obeying the call of God is a walk of faith. It is a journey with a definite purpose: God's purpose! He wants to draw all men unto Him. What a privilege that He—

> **...hath saved us, and called us with an holy calling, not according to our works, but according to his own purpose and grace,...**
>
> **2 Timothy 1:9**

Elijah's Walk of Obedience

The prophet Elijah was anointed by God for a special mission. He was called to deliver God's people from worshiping the demon-god Baal and to return them to Jehovah. He experienced some vital lessons that can benefit us in our walk of obedience. (I suggest you stop now and read 1 Kings, Chapter 17.)

Before the first verse of Chapter 17 there is no mention of Elijah in the Bible. We know only that he was a Tishbite from Gilead. We're not even sure that anyone was aware of his anointing. Yet, with complete authority he announces to the evil King Ahab—

> **...As surely as the Lord God of Israel lives—the God whom I worship and serve—there won't be any dew or rain for several years until I say the word!**
> **1 Kings 17:1**
> **The Living Bible**

Several lessons may be learned in this verse alone. First, the fact that God would call an obscure Tishbite from Gilead proves that **His choices are sovereign.**[28] If Elijah were to be raised up today, we'd need his credentials. We'd want to know what Bible school or seminary he attended. And if he wasn't from our ideological "camp," we probably wouldn't recognize his calling.

Praise God! He doesn't look at our abilities or our background. He chooses people just because He's God. And He makes decisions "...according to his own will" (Heb. 2:4). **A calling that's supported by an anointing has to come from God. You can't call yourself, and other men can't call you.**

Second, **Elijah spoke with authority**. He had a boldness that could come only from "knowing" what you've been called to. Elijah must have had an inward witness, confirming his assignment. Third, that **authority is always born in a time of private preparation**. The prophet was well prepared for this event, for he said, "...the God whom I worship and serve." Jesus Himself said—

> **Thou shalt worship the Lord God, and**
> **him only shalt thou serve.**
>
> **Matthew 4:10**

Worship always precedes service. Elijah was prepared to serve because he had spent time worshiping God, first. The time of preparation is out of the public eye, in the secret place with the Father. Remember, the anointing is increased through association (submission to a higher ministry), prayer and fasting, **praise and worship**, and periods of silence. (See Chapter 5.)

Paying the Price

Immediately after Elijah's proclamation, the Lord told him to go and **hide** at Cherith Brook by the Jordan River. The Hebrew word for Jordan means "death of the self-life."[29] God wanted him away from public attention, whether positive or negative. He didn't want Elijah puffed up because he had been used, nor did he desire to see him abused by unbelieving heathen.

You would expect that after such a strong

appearance, Elijah would become a recognized figure, very much in the public eye and very much in demand. But, if he had gone that route, it would have ended his ministry. God said, "Go hide!" **Elijah still had much to learn about dying to self. It is a price that must be paid for the anointing.** We must learn to die daily to our own ambitions and aspirations.

Though Elijah was separated, God sustained him. God met his needs. Notice that God didn't tell Elijah that the brook would eventually dry up. Elijah should have known it. After all, he had prophesied, "No rain!" Nevertheless Elijah trusted in God and not the brook. If Elijah had trusted in the provision instead of the provider, he would have felt that God had deserted him when the provision was gone. **We can't put our trust in other people, in our jobs, or in our ministries. We have to put our trust in God.**

When the brook dried up, God sent Elijah to Zarephath, which means "testing and refining."[30] God promised that a widow would feed him there, but when he arrived he found the woman and her son preparing their last meal before they starved to death. **Elijah was being tested.** Should he doubt that he had been sent? Was she the right woman? Was this the right city?

Instead of doubting, he encouraged the woman to give to God first, and trust God. The woman began to draw on his anointing. She believed he was anointed, she put a demand of faith on the anointing, and she was committed to Elijah's ministry. (See Chapter 5.) The widow received a **great** miracle because of her faith. Testing and refining produces—

> **...a vessel set apart and useful for honorable and noble purposes, consecrated and profitable to the Master, fit and ready for any good work.**
>
> **2 Timothy 2:21**
> **The Amplified Bible**

God tests us through our obedience. He doesn't put sickness or hardship on us to teach us. The devil is the thief that comes to steal, kill, and destroy (John 10:10). No one is exempt from testing. Luke 4:1 in the Living Bible says that even Jesus was "...urged by the Spirit out into the barren wastelands...where Satan tempted him..." Jesus was victorious over his tempter. He passed the test and conquered death so that we can be victorious too! As it was with Elijah and Jesus, a time of refining, of dying to self, and of paying the price is necessary to fulfill your call in the power of God's anointing.

Experience of Resurrection

Elijah's final test in Zarephath came when the widow's son died. God had a revelation for Elijah beyond anything that he had yet received.[31] As he threw himself over the boy's body, praying for life to return, he suddenly identified with the situation. **There must be a death, before there can be a resurrection!** To maintain his anointing and fulfill his ministry, the prophet had to experience a death to his "self" life.

The Apostle Paul said, "...I die daily" (1 Cor. 15:31). The Amplified says, "...I die to self." Jesus, of course, faced death to the fullest extent so that we might have life. In Elijah's case, the boy's resurrection became his own resurrection. Elijah went forth from this experience to annihilate more than 400 prophets of Baal. He accomplished his mission because he was willing to walk in obedience. He paid the price for the anointing!

Conclusion

It is an honor and a privilege to be called by God. It takes great courage and commitment to walk in the calling. Yes, there is a price to pay, but the rewards for obedience far outweigh any personal sacrifice. No amount of compromise could dissuade me from operating in the power of God's anointing. No words adequately describe my emotions when someone is set free and delivered because of my obedience and the anointing that follows. This walk of faith and power in the Holy Spirit is what I was destined for. Thank God, He equips us. Thank God, He empowers us. When God calls, He anoints!

End Notes

1. From the song, "It's the Anointing," by Jim Earl Swilley, Baracah Publishing Co., 1986. Used by permission.

2. *The Zondervan Pictorial Bible Dictionary,* edited by Merrill C. Tenney, Zondervan Publishing House, 1963.

3. See #1.

4. *Webster's Seventh New Collegiate Dictionary,* G. & C. Merriam Company, 1965.

5. See #2.

6. See #2.

7. See #4.

8. *The Exhaustive Concordance of the Bible: together with Dictionaries of the Hebrew and Greek Words of the original, with references to the English words:,* by James Strong, Riverside Book and Bible House, Iowa Falls, Iowa.

9. Suggested reading, *Why Tongues,* by Kenneth E. Hagin, Faith Library Publications, Rhema Bible Church, Tulsa, 1975.

10. See #4.

11. See #4.

12. See #4.

13. See #8.

14. From Don Blevin's Ministers Conference Syllabus, Louisville, Ky., 1982.

15. See #4.

16. See #8.

17. See #4.

18. This chapter is based on a section from the sermon notebook of Rev. Ed Cox (not in print).

19. See #4.

20. See #2.

21. See #4.

22. *The Westminster Dictionary of the Bible,* by John D. Davis, The Westminster Press, 1944.

23. *Clarke's Commentary,* by Adam Clark, Abingdon - Cokesbury Press.

24. See #2.

25. See #8.

26. See #4.

27. See #2.

28. *The Refiner's Fire,* Volume I, by T. Austin Sparks, World Challenge, Inc.

29. See #28.

30. See #28.

31. See #28.

About the Author

Cheryl Ingram is a unique talent. It has been said that Cheryl "does with her voice what Phil Driscoll does with his horn." She is a powerful and charismatic singer who at the same time can tenderly perform a ballad.

With skill and versatility, Cheryl flows in an anointing that ushers in the presence of God. Salvations, healings, and deliverances always occur. She believes for the miraculous as she sings prepared music and new songs, unrehearsed, from her spirit.

Cheryl is an ordained minister who operates in the office of a psalmist. She and her husband, Steve, have founded the School of the Psalmist, graduating students from all over the United States and many different nations. Their vision is to raise up and instruct others who will become psalmists, "...vessels of honor, sanctified, useful to the Master and prepared to do every good work" (2 Timothy 2:21).

The granddaughter of a minister, Cheryl was raised in Detroit, Michigan. Her rich heritage of Christian faith is the foundation of her ministry today. She is a recording artist with several releases in the contemporary market. Her teaching series deal with subjects such as the anointing, stirring up the gift, the priestly role, and many more. Singing or speaking, Cheryl is a dynamic minister of the Gospel of Jesus Christ.

Dear Reader,

While doing research for this book I spoke with many people who had wonderful testimonies and stories about the anointing; especially its transference and operation in families. If you have a testimony you'd like to share about the anointing please write to me at—

Ingram Ministries, Inc.
P.O. Box 820954
Fort Worth, TX 76182-0954

His Vessel for Service,

Cheryl Ingram

For a

FREE CATALOG
of
Music and Teaching Materials

write—

Steve and Cheryl Ingram Ministries

P O Box 10261
Daytona Beach FL   32120

(904) 322-0020 Office
(904) 322-0097 Fax

1-800-485-6231

Steve and Cheryl Ingram Ministries
Praise and Worship Resources

MUSIC... by Cheryl Ingram

Stir It Up (Cassette)	$10.00
Stir It Up (CD)	$14.00
Follow The Light (Cassette)	$10.00

INSTRUMENTALS... by Steve Ingram

Sounds of Love	$10.00
Sounds of Joy	$10.00
Sounds of Peace	$10.00

TEACHING TAPES...

By Cheryl Ingram

Priestly Role of the Psalmist	$15.00
Tabernacle of David	$10.00
Stir Up the Gift Within You	$10.00
When God Calls, He Anoints	$20.00

By Steve Ingram

Intro. into the Psalmist Ministry	$10.00
Excellence in Music Ministry	$15.00

By Steve and Cheryl Ingram

Psalms, Hymns & Spiritual Songs	$10.00

Order form on back

ORDER FORM

QUT.	DESCRIPTION	UNIT PRICE	TOTAL
*UNDER $25 $1.50 $25 - $50 2.00 $50 - $100 2.50 OVER $100 3.00	SUB TOTAL		
	SHIPPING *		
	TOTAL PRICE		

*FOREIGN PLEASE PAY IN U.S. DOLLARS

NAME_____

ADDRESS_____

CITY_____ STATE_____ ZIP_____

TO PLACE A MASTER CARD/VISA ORDER CAll: 1-800-635-6231